Brainstorming

Idea 1	Funny Connections
→ ←	← →

💡 Related topics

🐔 Puns

Characters

Joke

Setup

Punchline

MY JOKE OF THE DAY PLANNER

Write the joke(s) you plan to tell this week.

○ MONDAY

FUTURE JOKES

_____

_____

○ TUESDAY

_____

_____

_____

○ WEDNESDAY

BEST JOKES THIS WEEK

_____

○ THURSDAY

_____

_____

_____

○ FRIDAY

_____

_____

○ SATURDAY / SUNDAY

_____

_____

Brainstorming

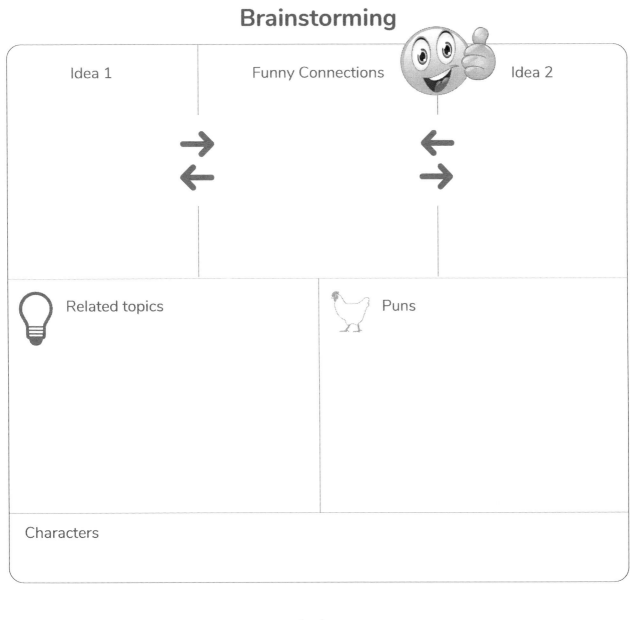

Idea 1	Funny Connections	Idea 2

Related topics

Puns

Characters

Joke

Setup

Punchline

MY JOKE OF THE DAY PLANNER

Write the joke(s) you plan to tell this week.

○ MONDAY

FUTURE JOKES

○ TUESDAY

○ WEDNESDAY

BEST JOKES THIS WEEK

○ THURSDAY

○ FRIDAY

○ SATURDAY / SUNDAY

Brainstorming

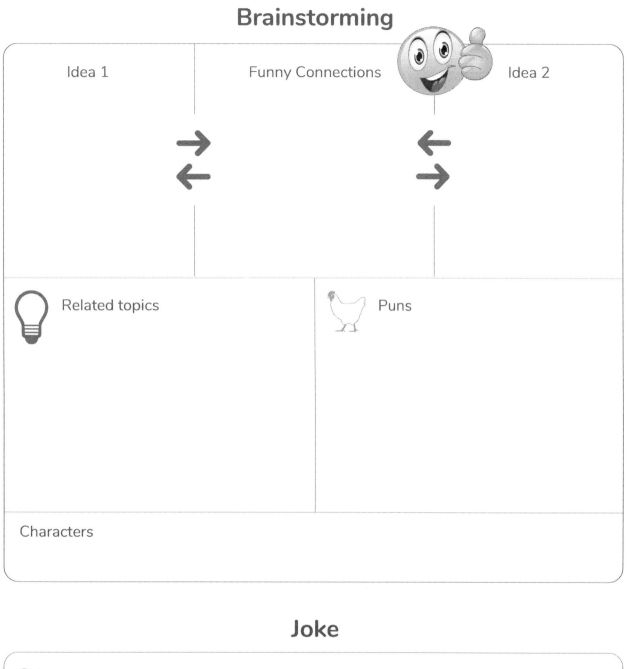

Idea 1

Funny Connections

Idea 2

Related topics

Puns

Characters

Joke

Setup

Punchline

MY JOKE OF THE DAY PLANNER

Write the joke(s) you plan to tell this week.

○ MONDAY

FUTURE JOKES

_____

_____

○ TUESDAY

_____

_____

_____

_____

○ WEDNESDAY

BEST JOKES THIS WEEK

_____

_____

○ THURSDAY

_____

_____

_____

○ FRIDAY

_____

_____

_____

○ SATURDAY / SUNDAY

_____

_____

Brainstorming

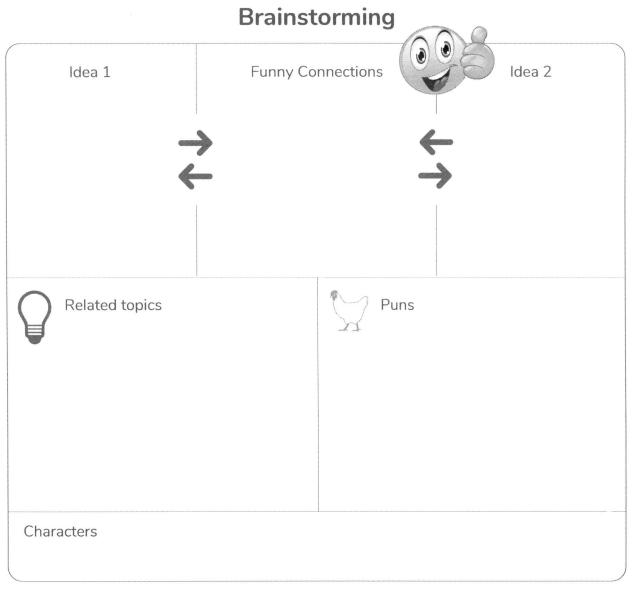

Idea 1   Funny Connections   Idea 2

Related topics

Puns

Characters

Joke

Setup

Punchline

MY JOKE OF THE DAY PLANNER

Write the joke(s) you plan to tell this week.

○ MONDAY

FUTURE JOKES

○ TUESDAY

○ WEDNESDAY

BEST JOKES THIS WEEK

○ THURSDAY

○ FRIDAY

○ SATURDAY / SUNDAY

Brainstorming

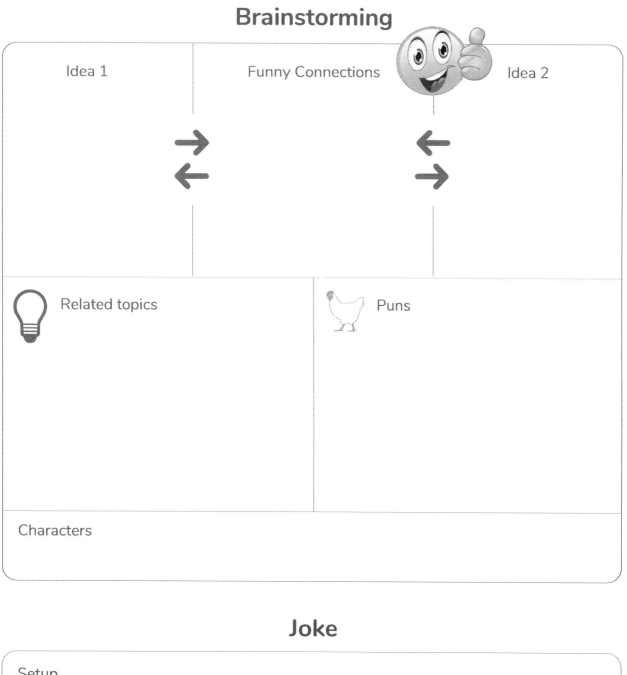

Idea 1

Funny Connections

Idea 2

💡 Related topics

🐔 Puns

Characters

Joke

Setup

Punchline

MY JOKE OF THE DAY PLANNER

Write the joke(s) you plan to tell this week.

○ MONDAY

_____

○ TUESDAY

_____

○ WEDNESDAY

_____

○ THURSDAY

_____

○ FRIDAY

_____

○ SATURDAY / SUNDAY

FUTURE JOKES

_____
_____
_____
_____
_____

BEST JOKES THIS WEEK

_____
_____
_____
_____
_____
_____
_____
_____
_____

Brainstorming

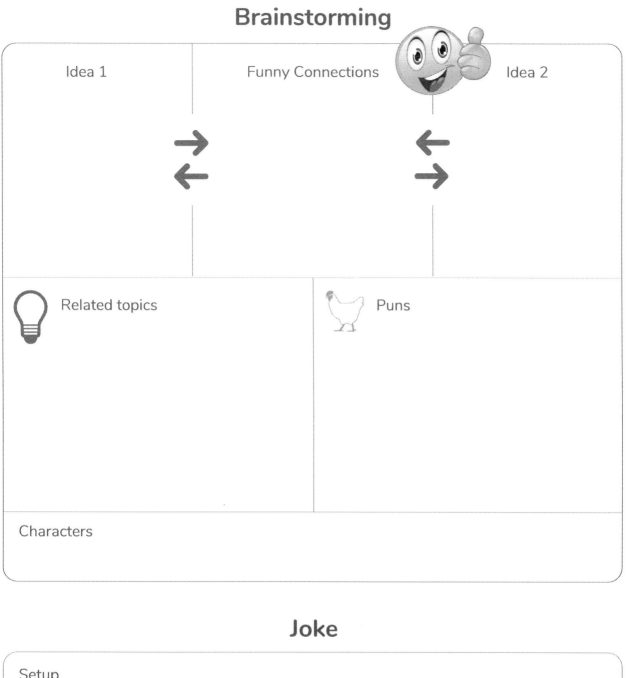

Idea 1	Funny Connections	Idea 2

Related topics

Puns

Characters

Joke

Setup

Punchline

MY JOKE OF THE DAY PLANNER

Write the joke(s) you plan to tell this week.

○ MONDAY

FUTURE JOKES

_____

_____

○ TUESDAY

_____

_____

_____

_____

○ WEDNESDAY

BEST JOKES THIS WEEK

_____

_____

○ THURSDAY

_____

_____

_____

_____

○ FRIDAY

_____

_____

_____

○ SATURDAY / SUNDAY

_____

_____

_____

Brainstorming

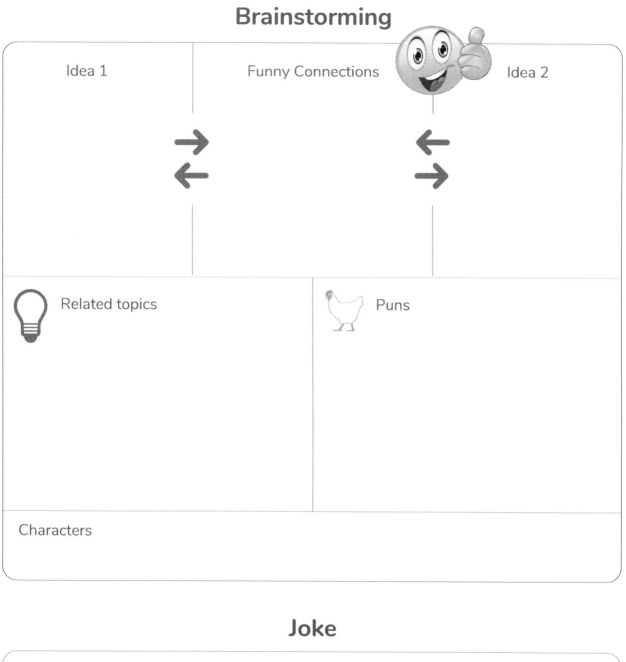

Idea 1

Funny Connections

Idea 2

Related topics

Puns

Characters

Joke

Setup

Punchline

MY JOKE OF THE DAY PLANNER

Write the joke(s) you plan to tell this week.

○ MONDAY

○ TUESDAY

○ WEDNESDAY

○ THURSDAY

○ FRIDAY

○ SATURDAY / SUNDAY

FUTURE JOKES

_____
_____
_____
_____
_____
_____

BEST JOKES THIS WEEK

_____
_____
_____
_____
_____
_____
_____
_____
_____

Brainstorming

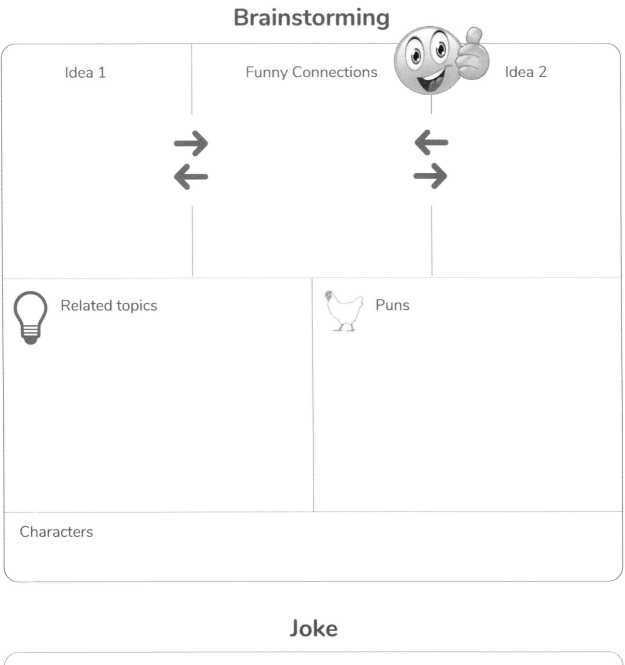

Idea 1	Funny Connections	Idea 2

Related topics

Puns

Characters

Joke

Setup

Punchline

MY JOKE OF THE DAY PLANNER

Write the joke(s) you plan to tell this week.

○ MONDAY

FUTURE JOKES

○ TUESDAY

○ WEDNESDAY

BEST JOKES THIS WEEK

○ THURSDAY

○ FRIDAY

○ SATURDAY / SUNDAY

Brainstorming

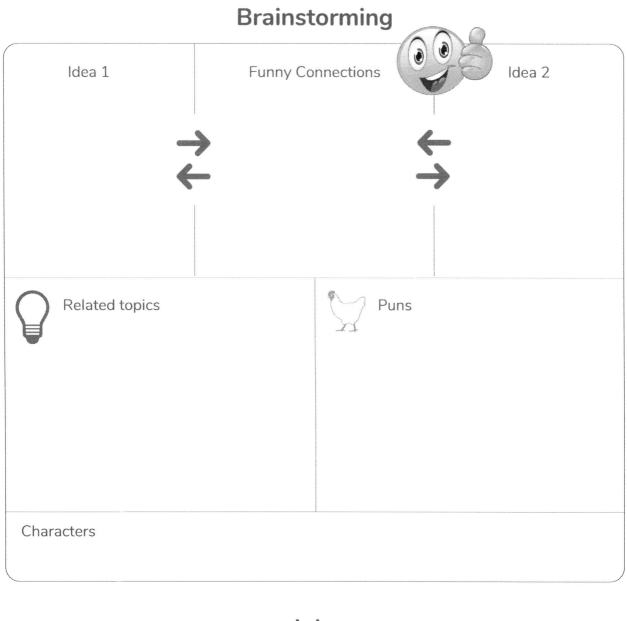

Idea 1   Funny Connections   Idea 2

Related topics

Puns

Characters

Joke

Setup

Punchline

MY JOKE OF THE DAY PLANNER

Write the joke(s) you plan to tell this week.

○ MONDAY

FUTURE JOKES

_____

○ TUESDAY

_____

_____

_____

_____

○ WEDNESDAY

BEST JOKES THIS WEEK

_____

_____

○ THURSDAY

_____

_____

_____

_____

○ FRIDAY

_____

_____

_____

○ SATURDAY / SUNDAY

_____

_____

_____

Brainstorming

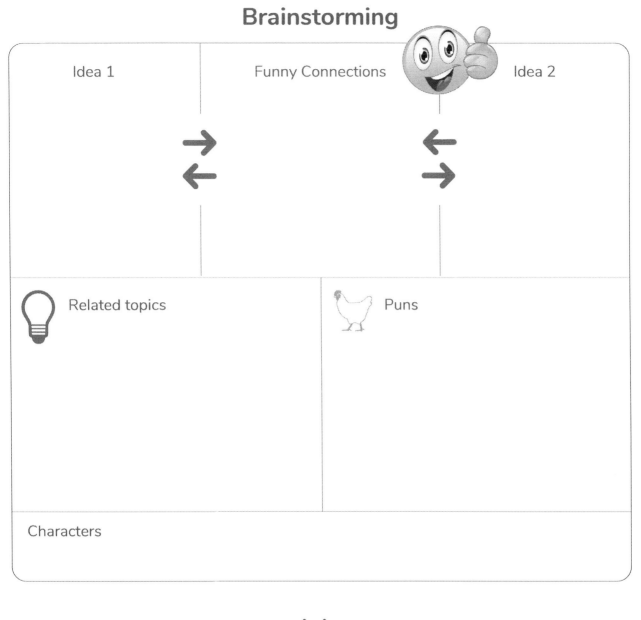

| Idea 1 | Funny Connections | Idea 2 |

Related topics

Puns

Characters

Joke

Setup

Punchline

MY JOKE OF THE DAY PLANNER

Write the joke(s) you plan to tell this week.

○ MONDAY

FUTURE JOKES

_____ _____

_____

○ TUESDAY

_____

_____

_____

○ WEDNESDAY

_____

BEST JOKES THIS WEEK

_____

_____

○ THURSDAY

_____

_____

_____

○ FRIDAY

_____

_____

_____

○ SATURDAY / SUNDAY

_____

_____

Brainstorming

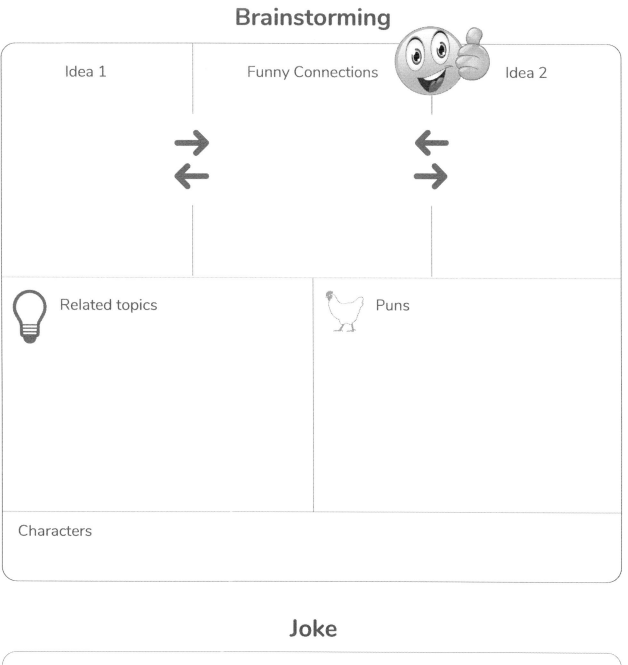

Idea 1

Funny Connections

Idea 2

Related topics

Puns

Characters

Joke

Setup

Punchline

MY JOKE OF THE DAY PLANNER

Write the joke(s) you plan to tell this week.

○ MONDAY

_____

○ TUESDAY

_____

○ WEDNESDAY

_____

○ THURSDAY

_____

○ FRIDAY

_____

○ SATURDAY / SUNDAY

_____

FUTURE JOKES

_____
_____
_____
_____
_____

BEST JOKES THIS WEEK

_____
_____
_____
_____
_____
_____
_____
_____

Brainstorming

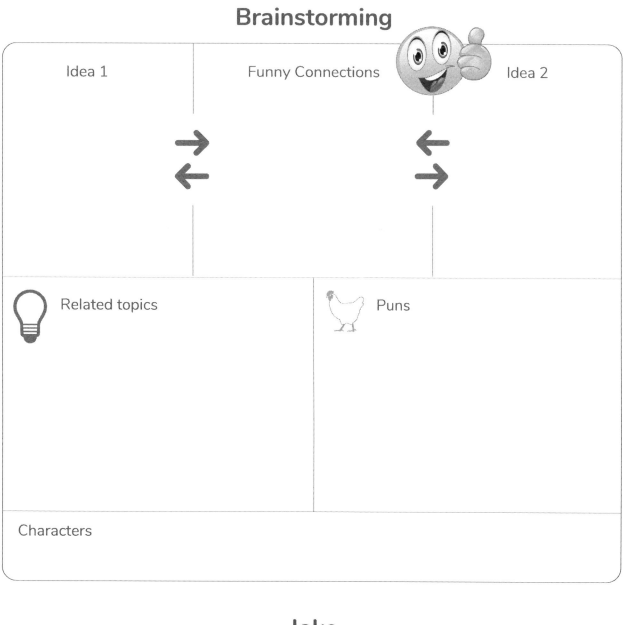

Idea 1	Funny Connections	Idea 2

Related topics

Puns

Characters

Joke

Setup

Punchline

MY JOKE OF THE DAY PLANNER

Write the joke(s) you plan to tell this week.

○ MONDAY

FUTURE JOKES

○ TUESDAY

○ WEDNESDAY

BEST JOKES THIS WEEK

○ THURSDAY

○ FRIDAY

○ SATURDAY / SUNDAY

Brainstorming

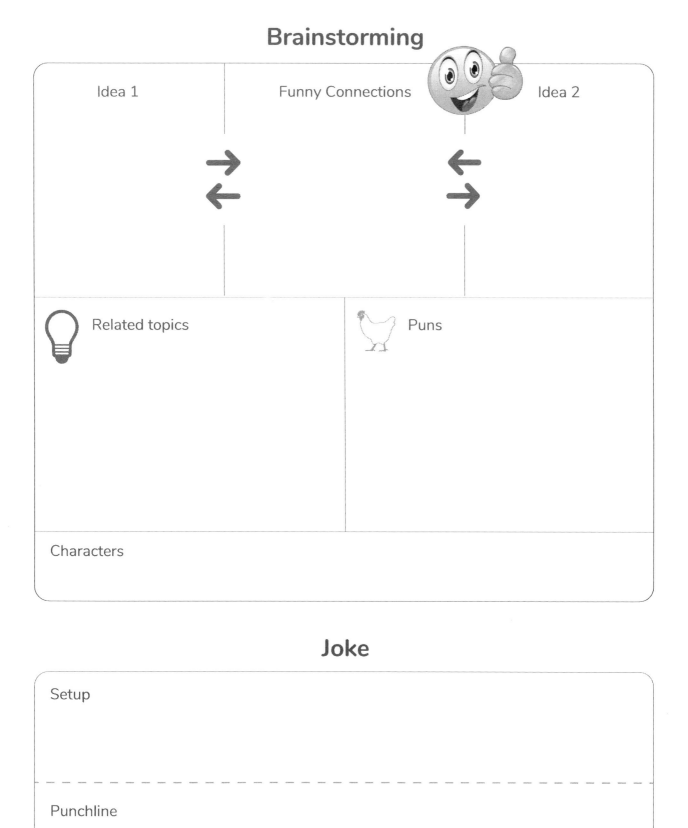

Idea 1

Funny Connections

Idea 2

Related topics

Puns

Characters

Joke

Setup

Punchline

MY JOKE OF THE DAY PLANNER

Write the joke(s) you plan to tell this week.

○ MONDAY

FUTURE JOKES

○ TUESDAY

○ WEDNESDAY

BEST JOKES THIS WEEK

○ THURSDAY

○ FRIDAY

○ SATURDAY / SUNDAY

Brainstorming

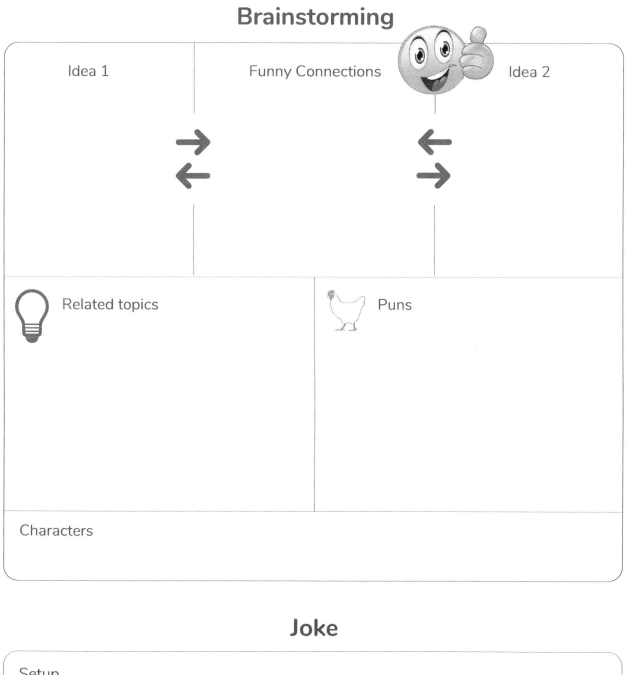

Idea 1

Funny Connections

Idea 2

Related topics

Puns

Characters

Joke

Setup

Punchline

MY JOKE OF THE DAY PLANNER

Write the joke(s) you plan to tell this week.

○ MONDAY

FUTURE JOKES

○ TUESDAY

○ WEDNESDAY

BEST JOKES THIS WEEK

○ THURSDAY

○ FRIDAY

○ SATURDAY / SUNDAY

Brainstorming

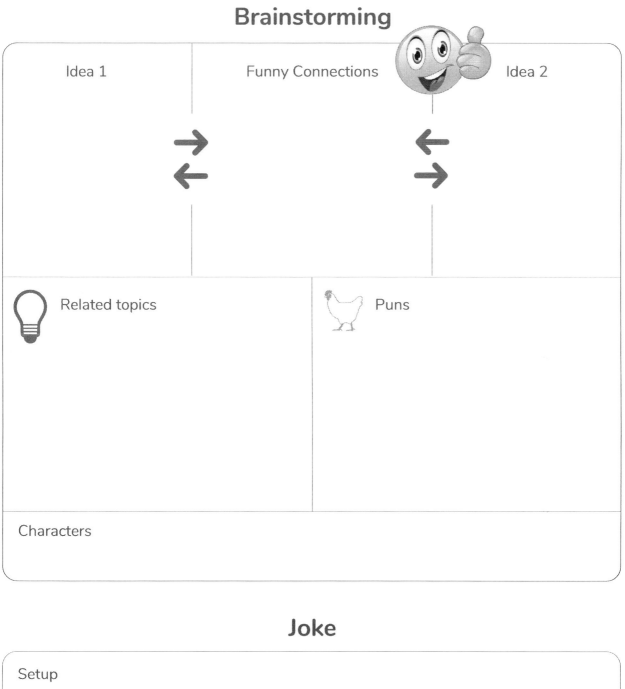

Idea 1   Funny Connections   Idea 2

Related topics

Puns

Characters

Joke

Setup

Punchline

MY JOKE OF THE DAY PLANNER

Write the joke(s) you plan to tell this week.

○ MONDAY

FUTURE JOKES

○ TUESDAY

○ WEDNESDAY

BEST JOKES THIS WEEK

○ THURSDAY

○ FRIDAY

○ SATURDAY / SUNDAY

Brainstorming

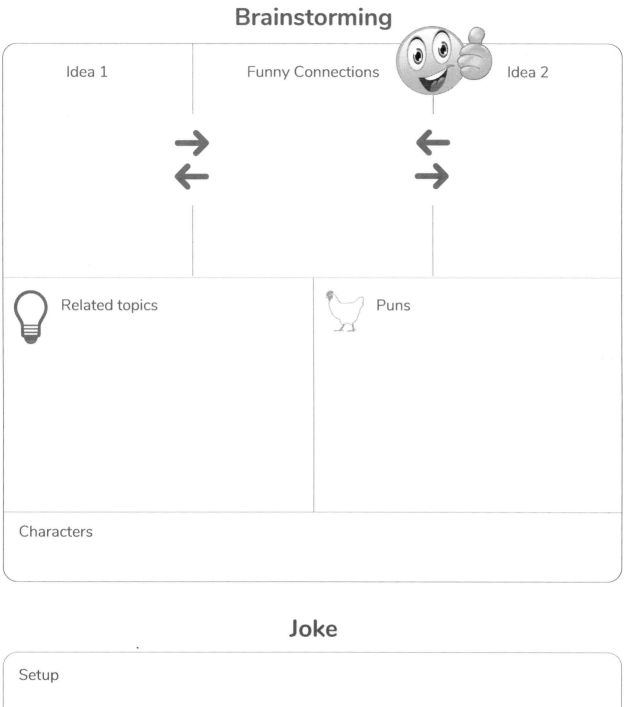

Idea 1　　　　Funny Connections　　　　Idea 2

Related topics

Puns

Characters

Joke

Setup

Punchline

MY JOKE OF THE DAY PLANNER

Write the joke(s) you plan to tell this week.

○ MONDAY

FUTURE JOKES

○ TUESDAY

○ WEDNESDAY

BEST JOKES THIS WEEK

○ THURSDAY

○ FRIDAY

○ SATURDAY / SUNDAY

Brainstorming

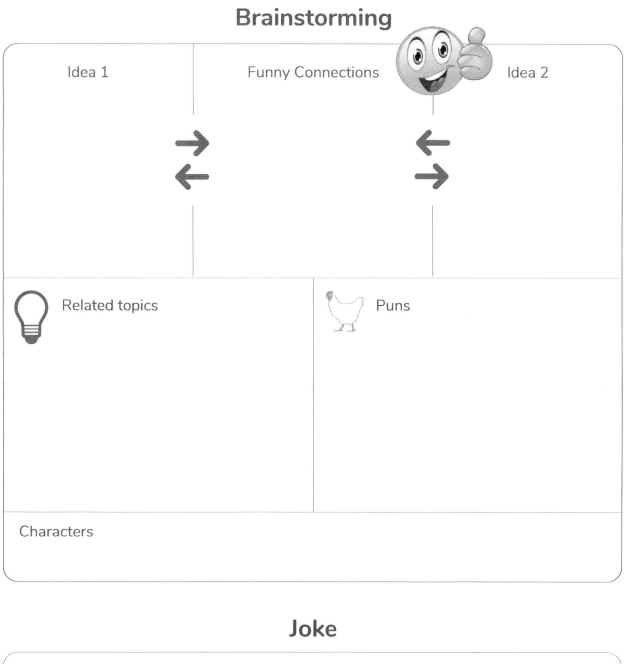

Idea 1	Funny Connections	Idea 2

Related topics

Puns

Characters

Joke

Setup

Punchline

MY JOKE OF THE DAY PLANNER

Write the joke(s) you plan to tell this week.

○ MONDAY

○ TUESDAY

○ WEDNESDAY

○ THURSDAY

○ FRIDAY

○ SATURDAY / SUNDAY

FUTURE JOKES

_____
_____
_____
_____
_____
_____
_____

BEST JOKES THIS WEEK

_____
_____
_____
_____
_____
_____
_____
_____
_____
_____

Brainstorming

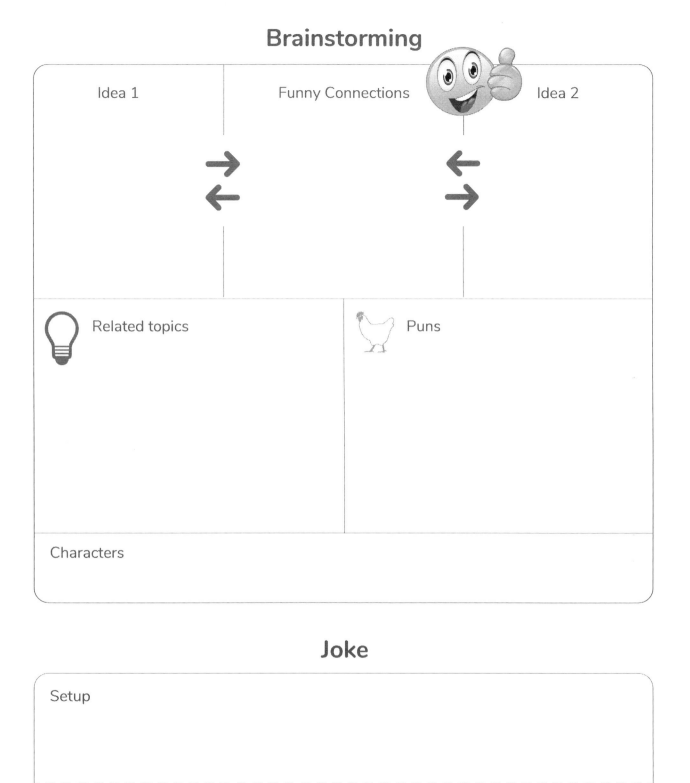

Idea 1   Funny Connections   Idea 2

Related topics

Puns

Characters

Joke

Setup

Punchline

MY JOKE OF THE DAY PLANNER

Write the joke(s) you plan to tell this week.

○ MONDAY

FUTURE JOKES

_____

_____

○ TUESDAY

_____

_____

_____

_____

○ WEDNESDAY

BEST JOKES THIS WEEK

_____

_____

○ THURSDAY

_____

_____

_____

○ FRIDAY

_____

_____

_____

○ SATURDAY / SUNDAY

_____

Brainstorming

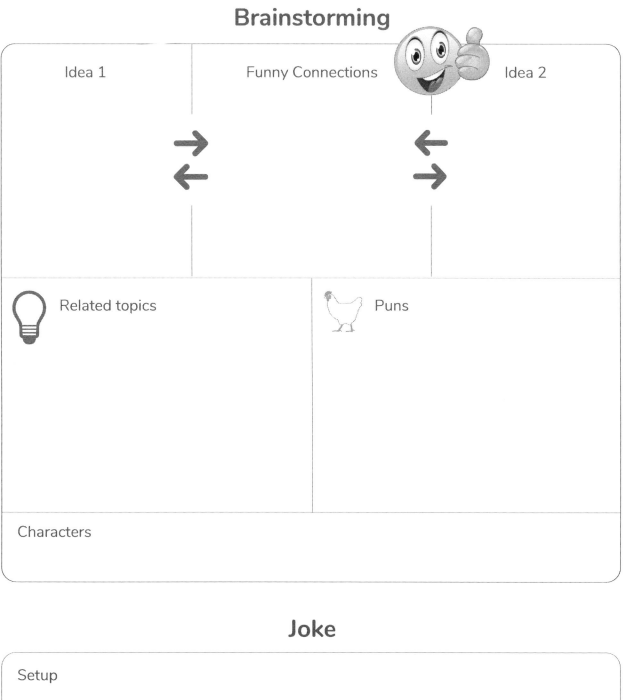

Idea 1   Funny Connections   Idea 2

Related topics

Puns

Characters

Joke

Setup

Punchline

MY JOKE OF THE DAY PLANNER

Write the joke(s) you plan to tell this week.

○ MONDAY

FUTURE JOKES

○ TUESDAY

○ WEDNESDAY

BEST JOKES THIS WEEK

○ THURSDAY

○ FRIDAY

○ SATURDAY / SUNDAY

Brainstorming

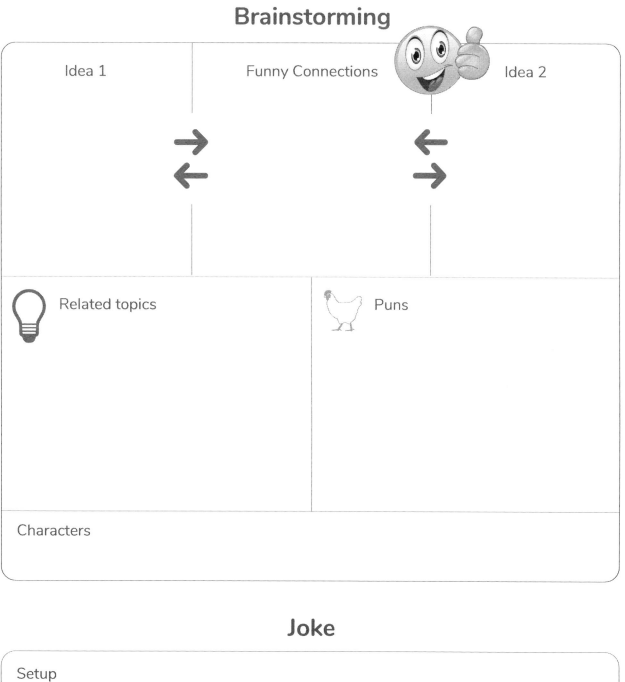

Idea 1	Funny Connections	Idea 2

Related topics

Puns

Characters

Joke

Setup

Punchline

MY JOKE OF THE DAY PLANNER

Write the joke(s) you plan to tell this week.

○ MONDAY

FUTURE JOKES

○ TUESDAY

○ WEDNESDAY

BEST JOKES THIS WEEK

○ THURSDAY

○ FRIDAY

○ SATURDAY / SUNDAY

Brainstorming

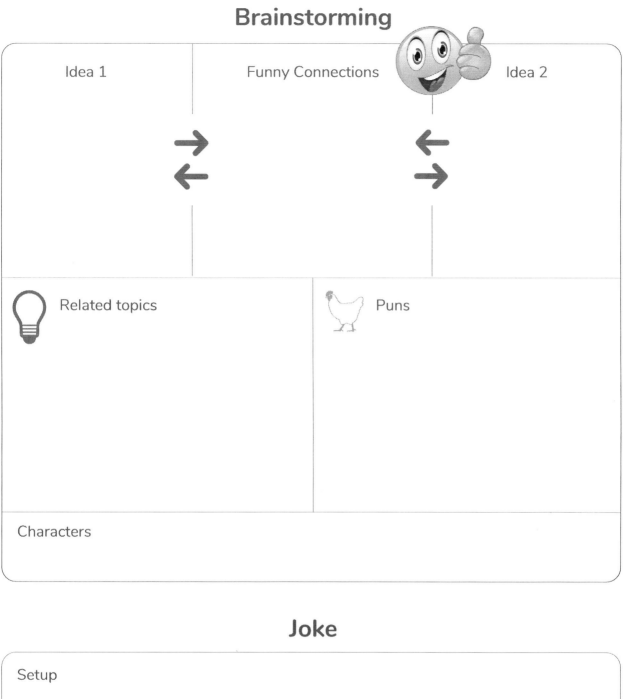

Idea 1

Funny Connections

Idea 2

Related topics

Puns

Characters

Joke

Setup

Punchline

MY JOKE OF THE DAY PLANNER

Write the joke(s) you plan to tell this week.

○ MONDAY

FUTURE JOKES

○ TUESDAY

○ WEDNESDAY

BEST JOKES THIS WEEK

○ THURSDAY

○ FRIDAY

○ SATURDAY / SUNDAY

Brainstorming

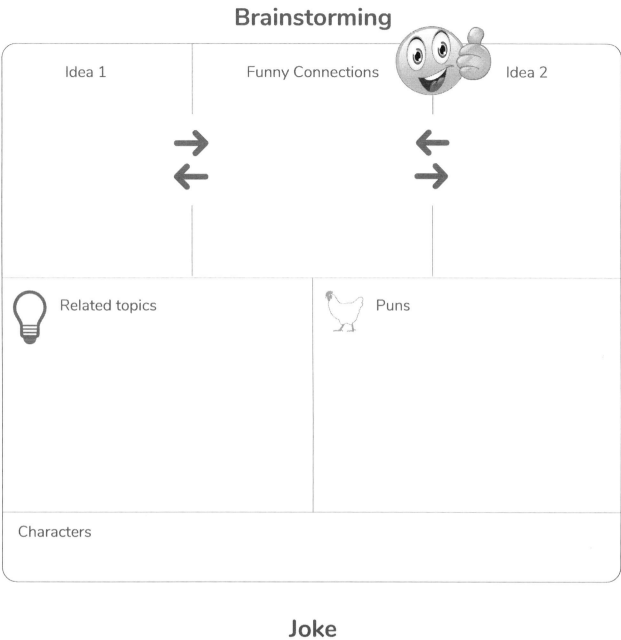

Idea 1	Funny Connections	Idea 2

Related topics

Puns

Characters

Joke

Setup

Punchline

MY JOKE OF THE DAY PLANNER

Write the joke(s) you plan to tell this week.

○ MONDAY

FUTURE JOKES

○ TUESDAY

○ WEDNESDAY

BEST JOKES THIS WEEK

○ THURSDAY

○ FRIDAY

○ SATURDAY / SUNDAY

Brainstorming

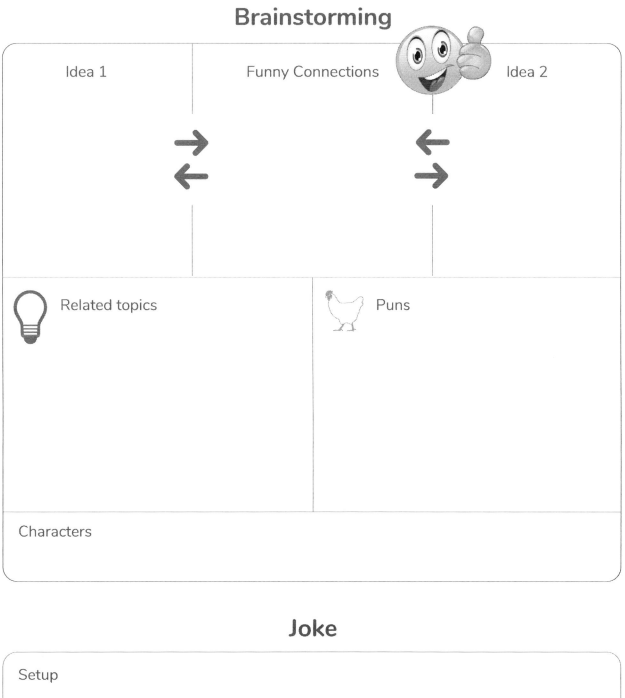

Idea 1   Funny Connections   Idea 2

Related topics

Puns

Characters

Joke

Setup

Punchline

MY JOKE OF THE DAY PLANNER

Write the joke(s) you plan to tell this week.

○ MONDAY

○ TUESDAY

○ WEDNESDAY

○ THURSDAY

○ FRIDAY

○ SATURDAY / SUNDAY

FUTURE JOKES

BEST JOKES THIS WEEK

Brainstorming

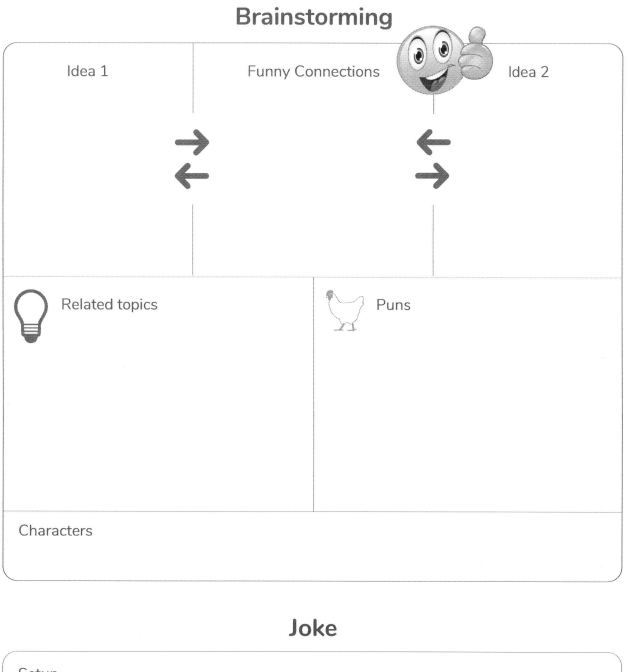

Idea 1	Funny Connections	Idea 2

Related topics

Puns

Characters

Joke

Setup

Punchline

MY JOKE OF THE DAY PLANNER

Write the joke(s) you plan to tell this week.

○ MONDAY

FUTURE JOKES

○ TUESDAY

○ WEDNESDAY

BEST JOKES THIS WEEK

○ THURSDAY

○ FRIDAY

○ SATURDAY / SUNDAY

Brainstorming

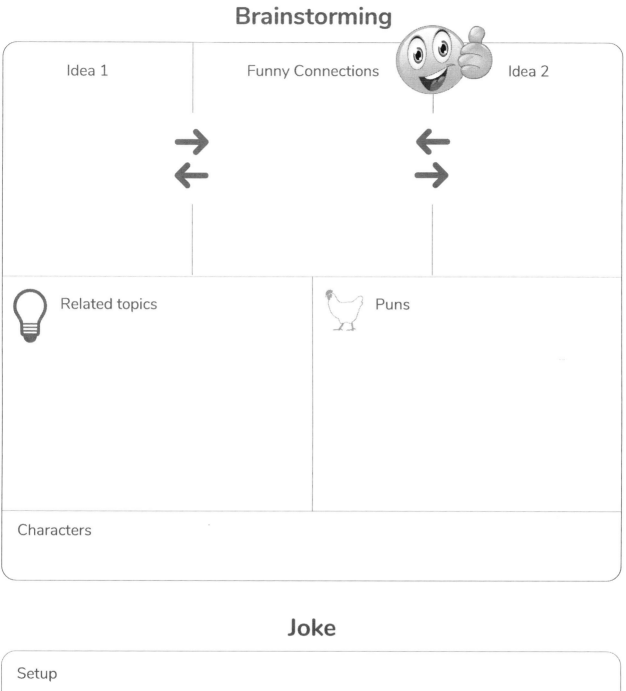

Idea 1	Funny Connections	Idea 2

Related topics

Puns

Characters

Joke

Setup

- -

Punchline

MY JOKE OF THE DAY PLANNER

Write the joke(s) you plan to tell this week.

○ MONDAY

FUTURE JOKES

○ TUESDAY

○ WEDNESDAY

BEST JOKES THIS WEEK

○ THURSDAY

○ FRIDAY

○ SATURDAY / SUNDAY

Brainstorming

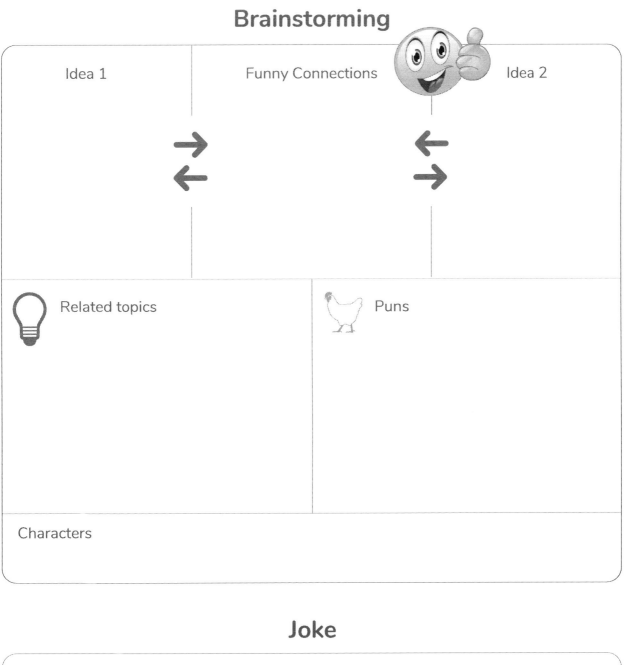

Idea 1	Funny Connections	Idea 2

Related topics

Puns

Characters

Joke

Setup

Punchline

MY JOKE OF THE DAY PLANNER

Write the joke(s) you plan to tell this week.

○ MONDAY

○ TUESDAY

○ WEDNESDAY

○ THURSDAY

○ FRIDAY

○ SATURDAY / SUNDAY

FUTURE JOKES

BEST JOKES THIS WEEK

Brainstorming

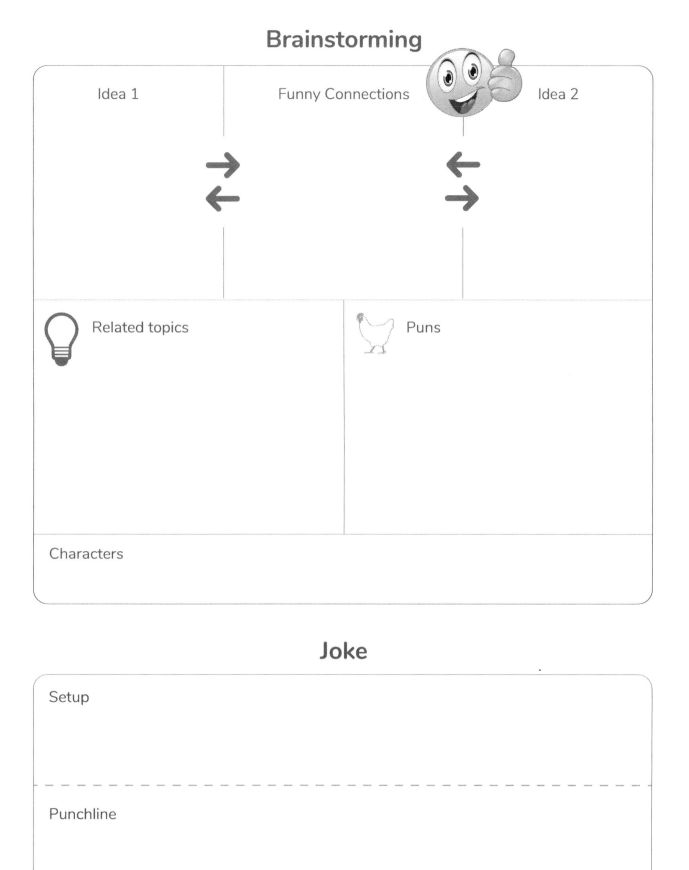

| Idea 1 | Funny Connections | Idea 2 |

Related topics

Puns

Characters

Joke

Setup

Punchline

MY JOKE OF THE DAY PLANNER

Write the joke(s) you plan to tell this week.

○ MONDAY

FUTURE JOKES

○ TUESDAY

○ WEDNESDAY

BEST JOKES THIS WEEK

○ THURSDAY

○ FRIDAY

○ SATURDAY / SUNDAY

Brainstorming

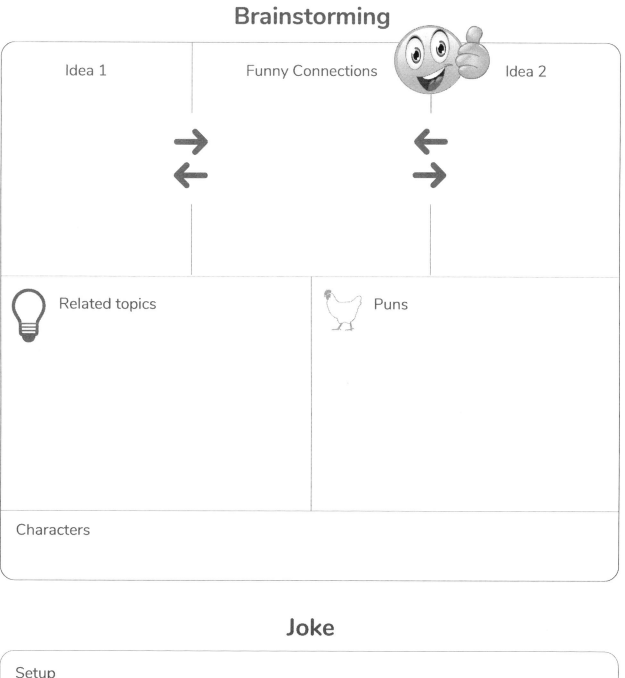

Idea 1

Funny Connections

Idea 2

Related topics

Puns

Characters

Joke

Setup

Punchline

MY JOKE OF THE DAY PLANNER

Write the joke(s) you plan to tell this week.

○ MONDAY

FUTURE JOKES

○ TUESDAY

○ WEDNESDAY

BEST JOKES THIS WEEK

○ THURSDAY

○ FRIDAY

○ SATURDAY / SUNDAY

Brainstorming

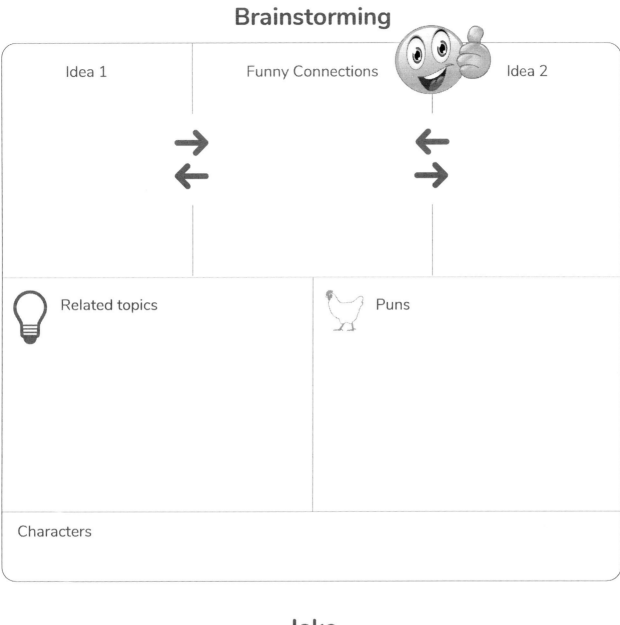

Idea 1   Funny Connections   Idea 2

Related topics

Puns

Characters

Joke

Setup

Punchline

MY JOKE OF THE DAY PLANNER

Write the joke(s) you plan to tell this week.

○ MONDAY

FUTURE JOKES

○ TUESDAY

○ WEDNESDAY

BEST JOKES THIS WEEK

○ THURSDAY

○ FRIDAY

○ SATURDAY / SUNDAY

Brainstorming

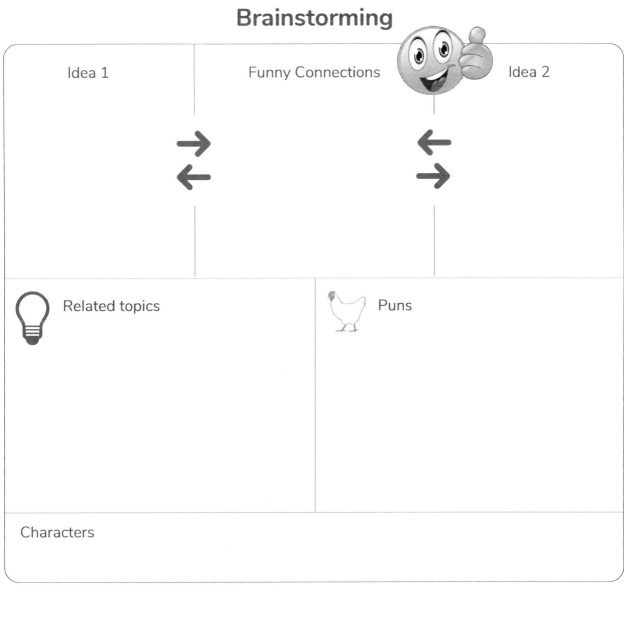

Idea 1

Funny Connections

Idea 2

Related topics

Puns

Characters

Joke

Setup

Punchline

MY JOKE OF THE DAY PLANNER

Write the joke(s) you plan to tell this week.

○ MONDAY

FUTURE JOKES

○ TUESDAY

○ WEDNESDAY

BEST JOKES THIS WEEK

○ THURSDAY

○ FRIDAY

○ SATURDAY / SUNDAY

Brainstorming

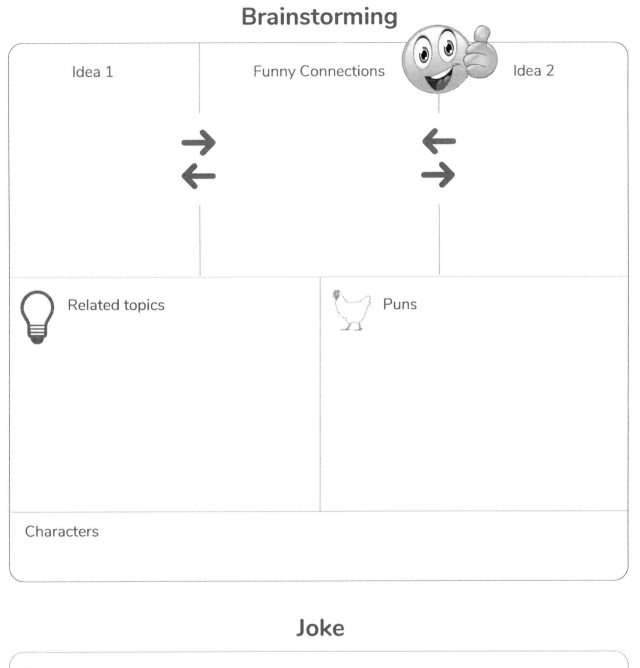

Idea 1

Funny Connections

Idea 2

Related topics

Puns

Characters

Joke

Setup

Punchline

MY JOKE OF THE DAY PLANNER

Write the joke(s) you plan to tell this week.

○ MONDAY

○ TUESDAY

○ WEDNESDAY

○ THURSDAY

○ FRIDAY

○ SATURDAY / SUNDAY

FUTURE JOKES

BEST JOKES THIS WEEK

Brainstorming

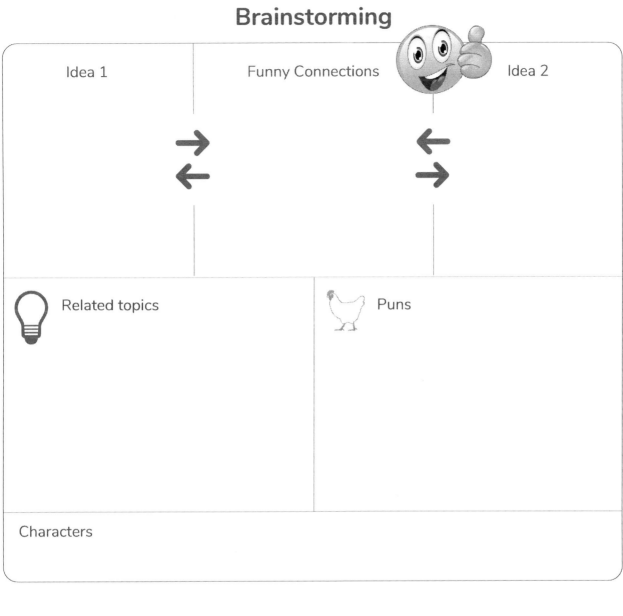

Idea 1

Funny Connections

Idea 2

Related topics

Puns

Characters

Joke

Setup

Punchline

MY JOKE OF THE DAY PLANNER

Write the joke(s) you plan to tell this week.

○ MONDAY

○ TUESDAY

○ WEDNESDAY

○ THURSDAY

○ FRIDAY

○ SATURDAY / SUNDAY

FUTURE JOKES

BEST JOKES THIS WEEK

Brainstorming

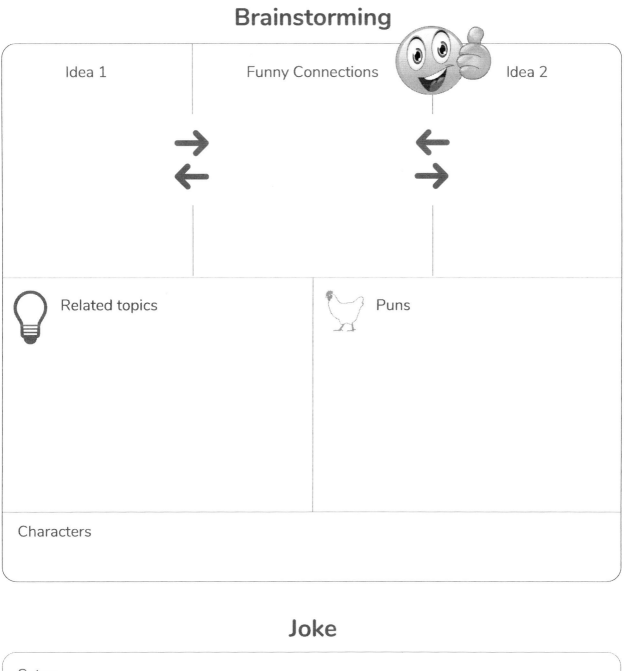

Idea 1	Funny Connections	Idea 2

Related topics

Puns

Characters

Joke

Setup

Punchline

MY JOKE OF THE DAY PLANNER

Write the joke(s) you plan to tell this week.

○ MONDAY

FUTURE JOKES

○ TUESDAY

○ WEDNESDAY

BEST JOKES THIS WEEK

○ THURSDAY

○ FRIDAY

○ SATURDAY / SUNDAY

Brainstorming

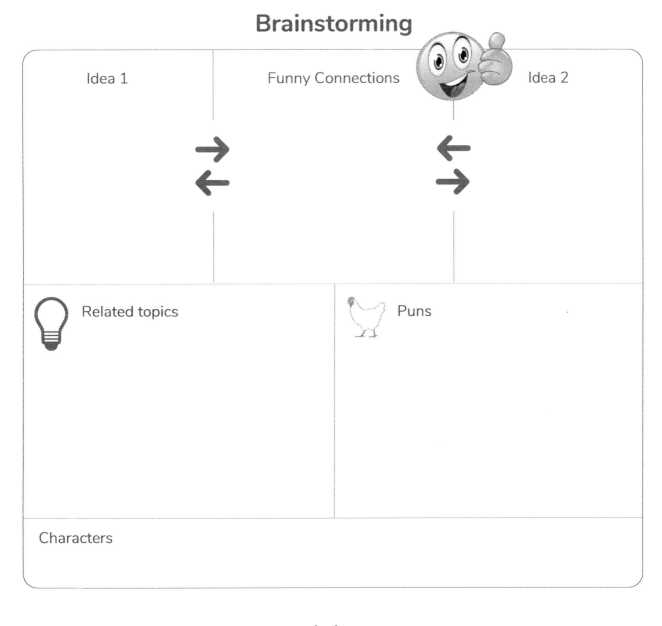

Idea 1	Funny Connections	Idea 2

Related topics

Puns

Characters

Joke

Setup

Punchline

MY JOKE OF THE DAY PLANNER

Write the joke(s) you plan to tell this week.

○ MONDAY

FUTURE JOKES

○ TUESDAY

○ WEDNESDAY

BEST JOKES THIS WEEK

○ THURSDAY

○ FRIDAY

○ SATURDAY / SUNDAY

Brainstorming

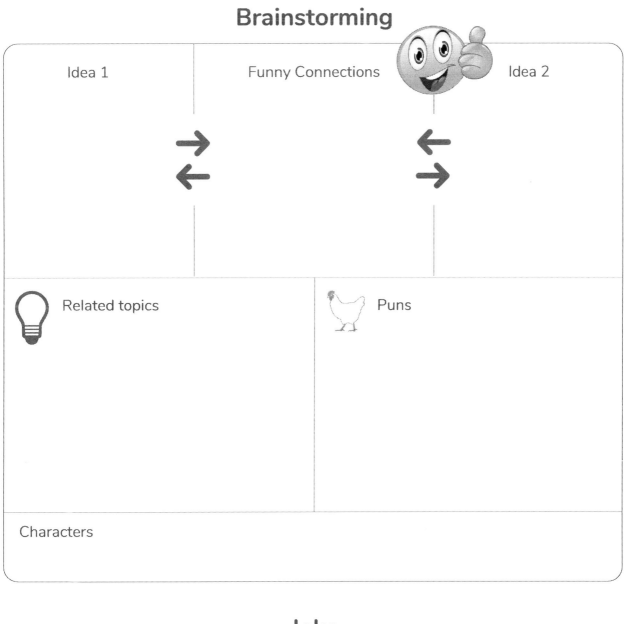

Idea 1	Funny Connections	Idea 2

Related topics

Puns

Characters

Joke

Setup

Punchline

MY JOKE OF THE DAY PLANNER

Write the joke(s) you plan to tell this week.

○ MONDAY

○ TUESDAY

○ WEDNESDAY

○ THURSDAY

○ FRIDAY

○ SATURDAY / SUNDAY

FUTURE JOKES

_____
_____
_____
_____
_____
_____

BEST JOKES THIS WEEK

_____
_____
_____
_____
_____
_____
_____
_____
_____
_____

Brainstorming

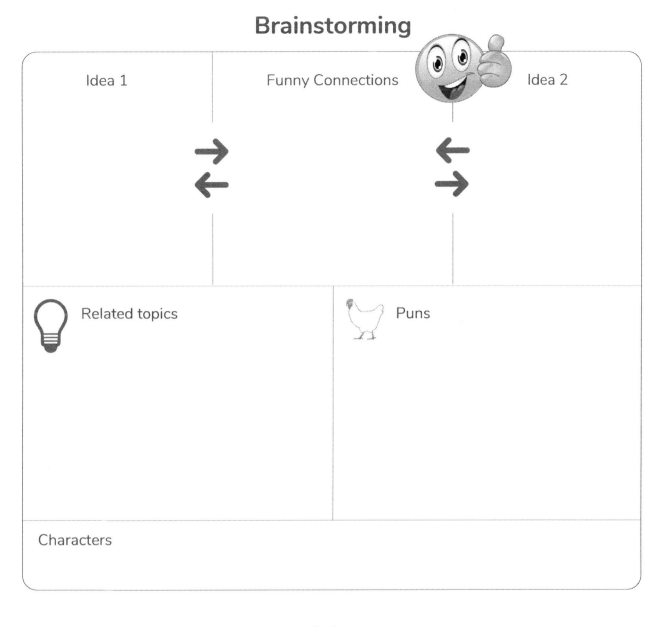

Idea 1	Funny Connections	Idea 2

Related topics

Puns

Characters

Joke

Setup

Punchline

MY JOKE OF THE DAY PLANNER

Write the joke(s) you plan to tell this week.

○ MONDAY

FUTURE JOKES

_____

_____

_____

○ TUESDAY

_____

_____

_____

_____

○ WEDNESDAY

BEST JOKES THIS WEEK

_____

_____

○ THURSDAY

_____

_____

_____

_____

○ FRIDAY

_____

_____

_____

○ SATURDAY / SUNDAY

_____

_____

_____

Brainstorming

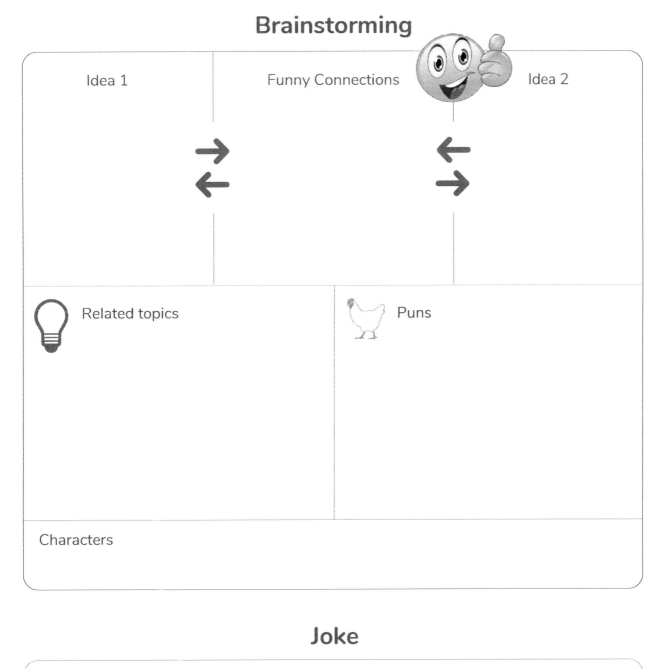

Idea 1

Funny Connections

Idea 2

Related topics

Puns

Characters

Joke

Setup

Punchline

MY JOKE OF THE DAY PLANNER

Write the joke(s) you plan to tell this week.

○ MONDAY

○ TUESDAY

○ WEDNESDAY

○ THURSDAY

○ FRIDAY

○ SATURDAY / SUNDAY

FUTURE JOKES

BEST JOKES THIS WEEK

Brainstorming

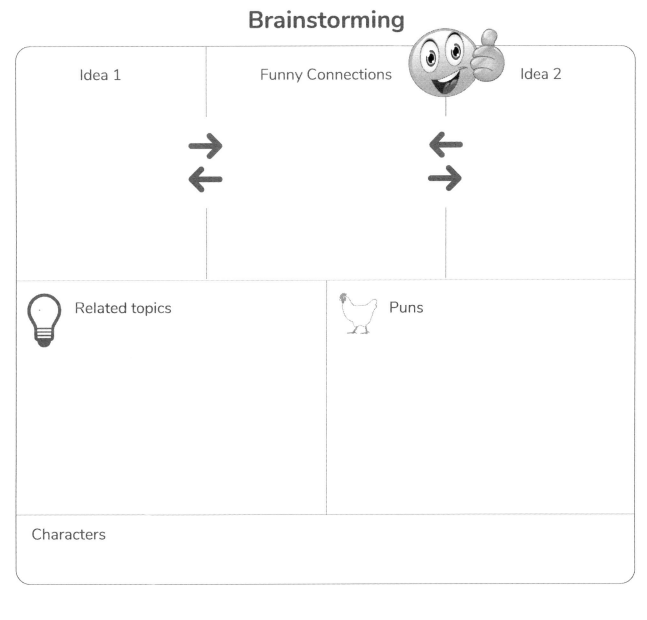

Idea 1	Funny Connections	Idea 2

Related topics

Puns

Characters

Joke

Setup

Punchline

MY JOKE OF THE DAY PLANNER

Write the joke(s) you plan to tell this week.

○ MONDAY

○ TUESDAY

○ WEDNESDAY

○ THURSDAY

○ FRIDAY

○ SATURDAY / SUNDAY

FUTURE JOKES

BEST JOKES THIS WEEK

Brainstorming

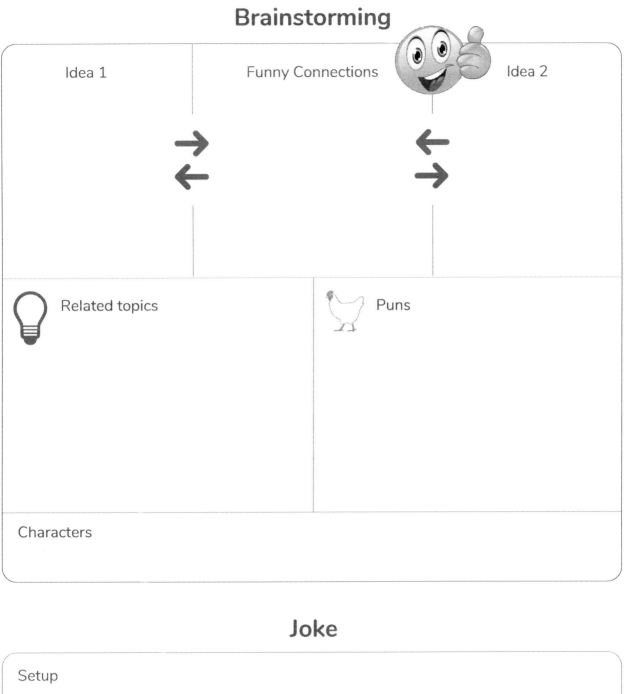

Idea 1	Funny Connections	Idea 2

Related topics

Puns

Characters

Joke

Setup

Punchline

MY JOKE OF THE DAY PLANNER

Write the joke(s) you plan to tell this week.

○ MONDAY

FUTURE JOKES

○ TUESDAY

○ WEDNESDAY

BEST JOKES THIS WEEK

○ THURSDAY

○ FRIDAY

○ SATURDAY / SUNDAY

Brainstorming

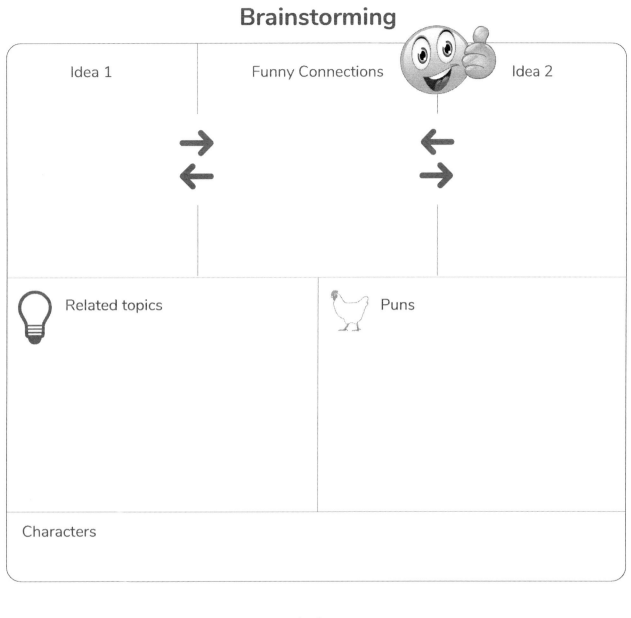

Idea 1	Funny Connections	Idea 2

Related topics

Puns

Characters

Joke

Setup

Punchline

MY JOKE OF THE DAY PLANNER

Write the joke(s) you plan to tell this week.

○ MONDAY

○ TUESDAY

○ WEDNESDAY

○ THURSDAY

○ FRIDAY

○ SATURDAY / SUNDAY

FUTURE JOKES

BEST JOKES THIS WEEK

Brainstorming

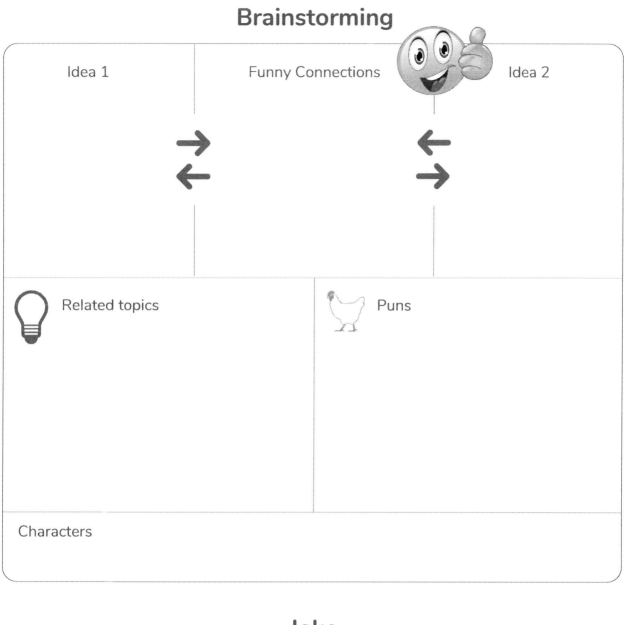

Idea 1	Funny Connections	Idea 2

Related topics

Puns

Characters

Joke

Setup

Punchline

MY JOKE OF THE DAY PLANNER

Write the joke(s) you plan to tell this week.

○ MONDAY

FUTURE JOKES

○ TUESDAY

○ WEDNESDAY

BEST JOKES THIS WEEK

○ THURSDAY

○ FRIDAY

○ SATURDAY / SUNDAY

Brainstorming

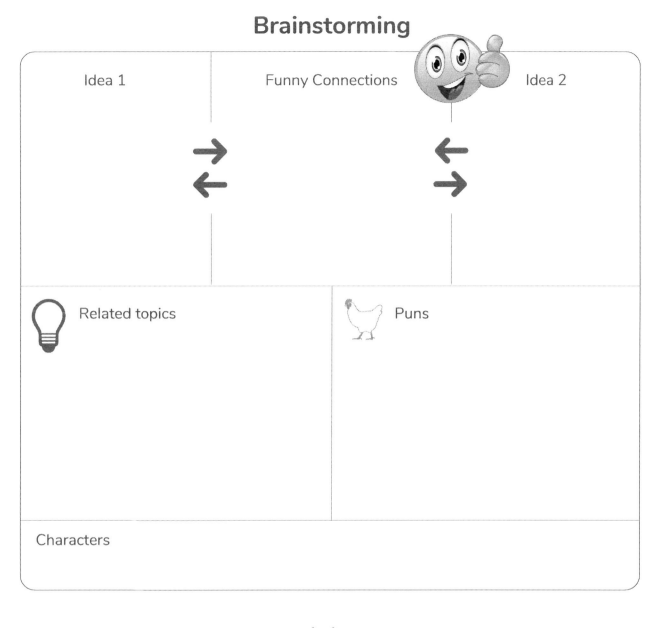

Idea 1	Funny Connections	Idea 2

Related topics

Puns

Characters

Joke

Setup

Punchline

MY JOKE OF THE DAY PLANNER

Write the joke(s) you plan to tell this week.

○ MONDAY

FUTURE JOKES

○ TUESDAY

○ WEDNESDAY

BEST JOKES THIS WEEK

○ THURSDAY

○ FRIDAY

○ SATURDAY / SUNDAY

Brainstorming

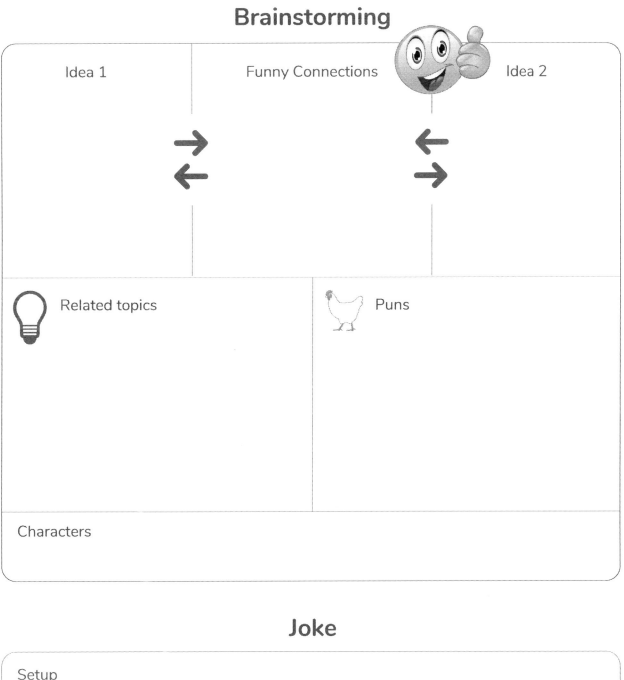

Idea 1	Funny Connections	Idea 2

💡 Related topics

🐔 Puns

Characters

Joke

Setup

Punchline

MY JOKE OF THE DAY PLANNER

Write the joke(s) you plan to tell this week.

○ MONDAY

FUTURE JOKES

○ TUESDAY

○ WEDNESDAY

BEST JOKES THIS WEEK

○ THURSDAY

○ FRIDAY

○ SATURDAY / SUNDAY

Brainstorming

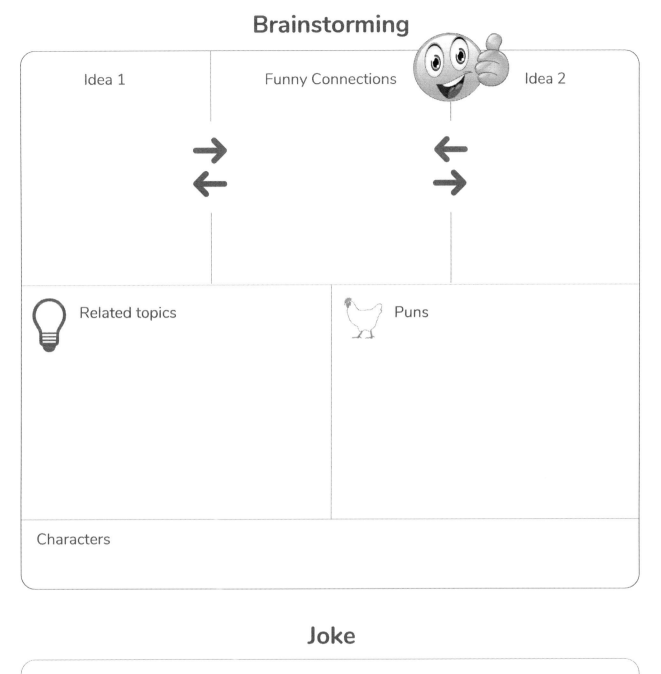

| Idea 1 | Funny Connections | Idea 2 |

Related topics

Puns

Characters

Joke

Setup

Punchline

MY JOKE OF THE DAY PLANNER

Write the joke(s) you plan to tell this week.

○ MONDAY

FUTURE JOKES

_____

_____

○ TUESDAY

_____

_____

_____

_____

_____

○ WEDNESDAY

BEST JOKES THIS WEEK

_____

○ THURSDAY

_____

_____

_____

_____

○ FRIDAY

_____

_____

_____

_____

○ SATURDAY / SUNDAY

_____

_____

_____

_____

Brainstorming

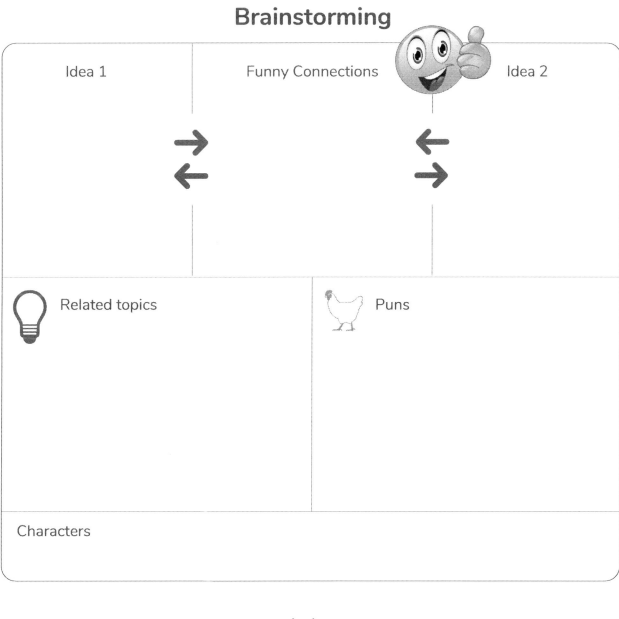

Idea 1

Funny Connections

Idea 2

💡 Related topics

🐔 Puns

Characters

Joke

Setup

Punchline

MY JOKE OF THE DAY PLANNER

Write the joke(s) you plan to tell this week.

○ MONDAY

FUTURE JOKES

_____

_____

○ TUESDAY

_____

_____

_____

○ WEDNESDAY

_____

BEST JOKES THIS WEEK

_____

○ THURSDAY

_____

_____

_____

_____

○ FRIDAY

_____

_____

_____

○ SATURDAY / SUNDAY

_____

_____

_____

Brainstorming

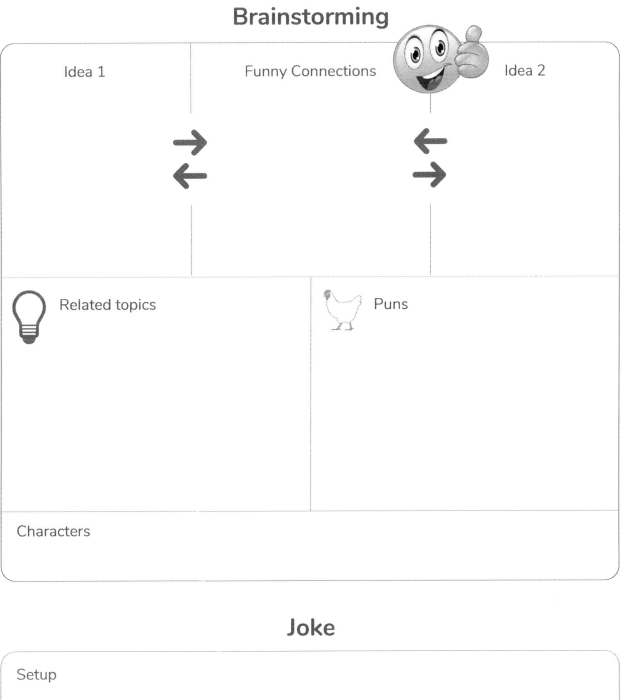

Idea 1	Funny Connections	Idea 2

💡 Related topics

🐔 Puns

Characters

Joke

Setup

Punchline

MY JOKE OF THE DAY PLANNER

Write the joke(s) you plan to tell this week.

○ MONDAY

FUTURE JOKES

_____

_____

○ TUESDAY

_____

_____

_____

_____

○ WEDNESDAY

BEST JOKES THIS WEEK

_____

○ THURSDAY

_____

_____

_____

○ FRIDAY

_____

_____

_____

○ SATURDAY / SUNDAY

_____

_____

_____

Brainstorming

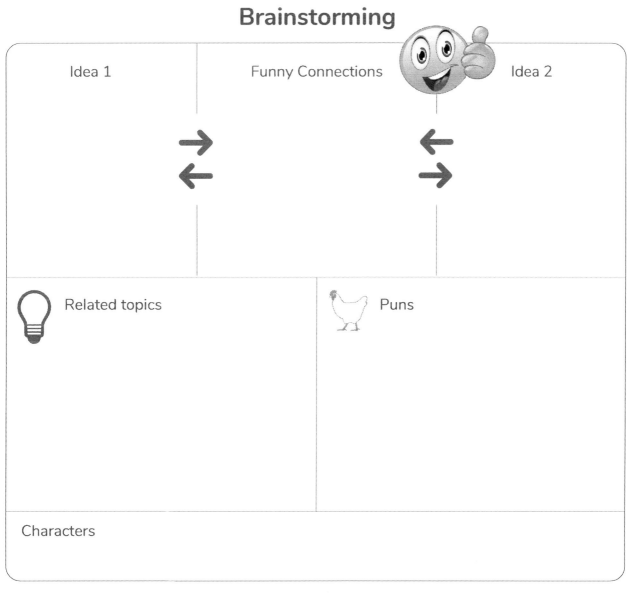

| Idea 1 | Funny Connections | Idea 2 |

Related topics

Puns

Characters

Joke

Setup

Punchline

MY JOKE OF THE DAY PLANNER

Write the joke(s) you plan to tell this week.

○ MONDAY

FUTURE JOKES

○ TUESDAY

○ WEDNESDAY

BEST JOKES THIS WEEK

○ THURSDAY

○ FRIDAY

○ SATURDAY / SUNDAY

Brainstorming

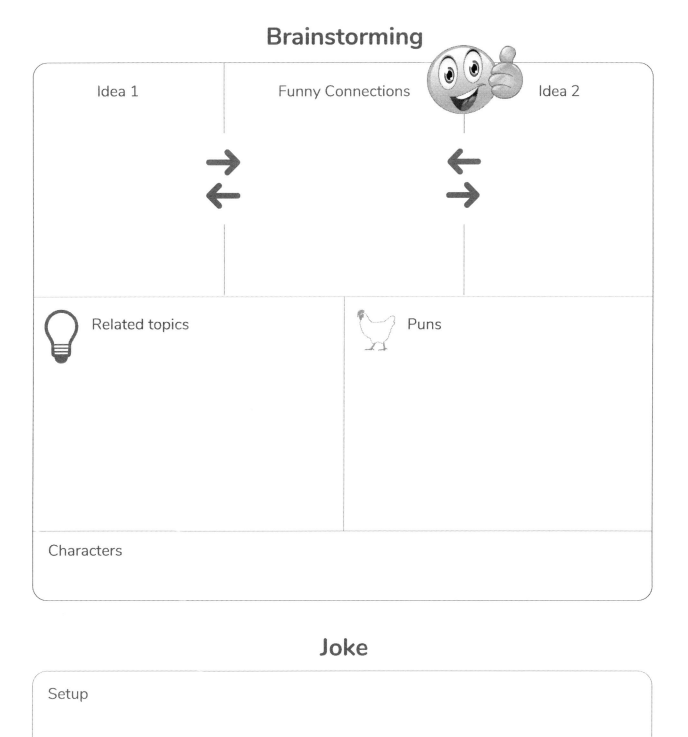

Idea 1   Funny Connections   Idea 2

Related topics

Puns

Characters

Joke

Setup

Punchline

MY JOKE OF THE DAY PLANNER

Write the joke(s) you plan to tell this week.

○ MONDAY

○ TUESDAY

○ WEDNESDAY

○ THURSDAY

○ FRIDAY

○ SATURDAY / SUNDAY

FUTURE JOKES

BEST JOKES THIS WEEK

Brainstorming

Idea 1

Funny Connections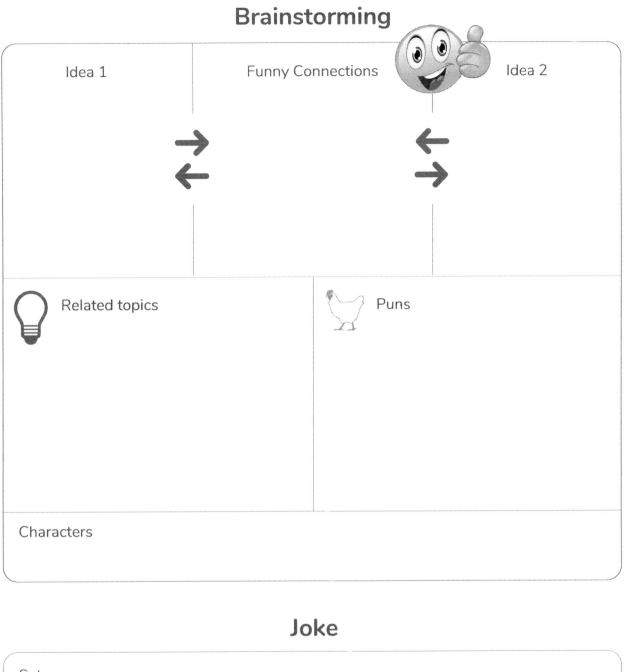

Idea 2

💡 Related topics

🐔 Puns

Characters

Joke

Setup

Punchline

MY JOKE OF THE DAY PLANNER

Write the joke(s) you plan to tell this week.

○ MONDAY

FUTURE JOKES

_____
_____
_____
_____
_____

○ TUESDAY

○ WEDNESDAY

BEST JOKES THIS WEEK

_____
_____
_____
_____
_____

○ THURSDAY

○ FRIDAY

○ SATURDAY / SUNDAY

Brainstorming

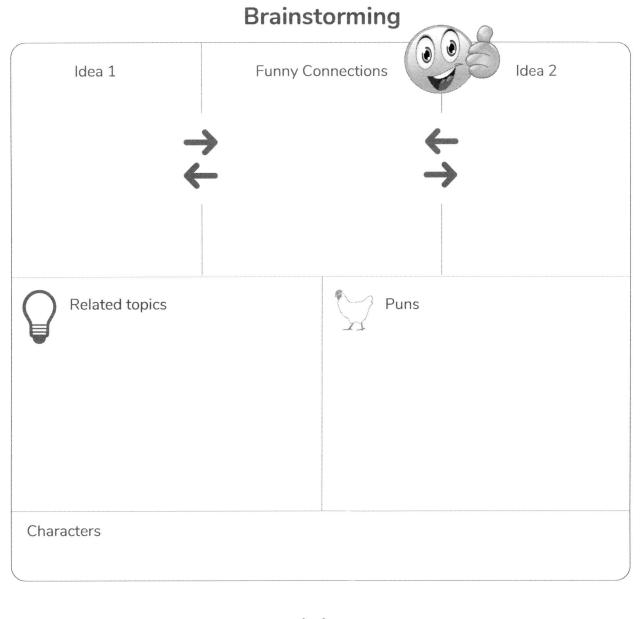

Idea 1

Funny Connections

Idea 2

Related topics

Puns

Characters

Joke

Setup

Punchline

MY JOKE OF THE DAY PLANNER

Write the joke(s) you plan to tell this week.

○ MONDAY

○ TUESDAY

○ WEDNESDAY

○ THURSDAY

○ FRIDAY

○ SATURDAY / SUNDAY

FUTURE JOKES

BEST JOKES THIS WEEK

Brainstorming

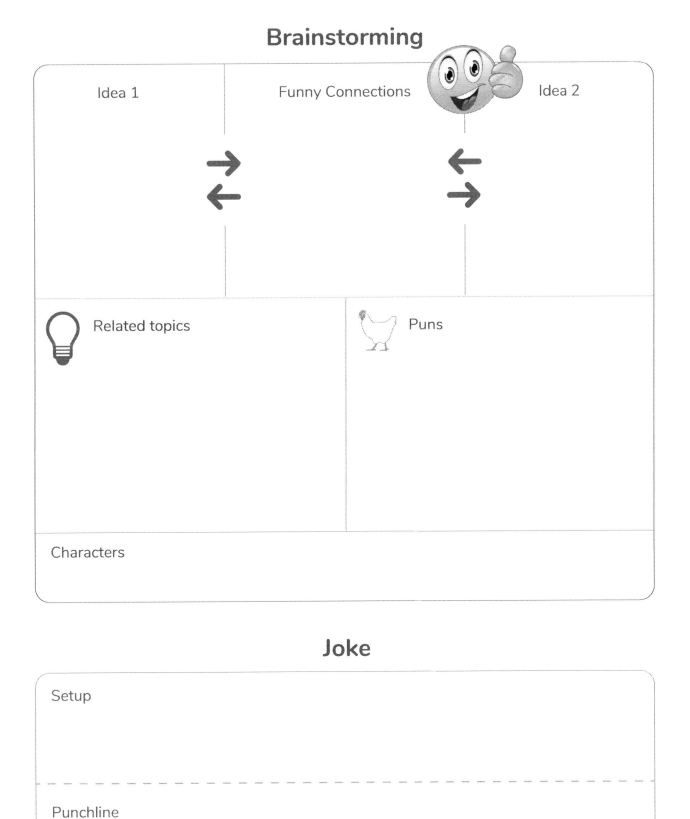

Idea 1

Funny Connections

Idea 2

Related topics

Puns

Characters

Joke

Setup

Punchline

MY JOKE OF THE DAY PLANNER

Write the joke(s) you plan to tell this week.

○ MONDAY

FUTURE JOKES

○ TUESDAY

○ WEDNESDAY

BEST JOKES THIS WEEK

○ THURSDAY

○ FRIDAY

○ SATURDAY / SUNDAY

Brainstorming

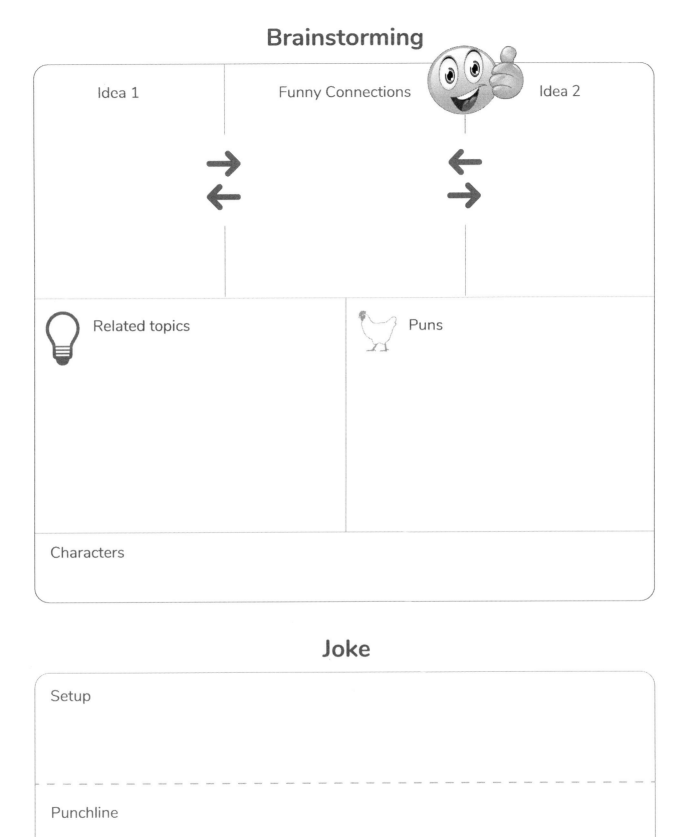

| Idea 1 | Funny Connections | Idea 2 |

Related topics

Puns

Characters

Joke

Setup

Punchline

MY JOKE OF THE DAY PLANNER

Write the joke(s) you plan to tell this week.

○ MONDAY

○ TUESDAY

○ WEDNESDAY

○ THURSDAY

○ FRIDAY

○ SATURDAY / SUNDAY

FUTURE JOKES

_____
_____
_____
_____
_____
_____

BEST JOKES THIS WEEK

_____
_____
_____
_____
_____
_____
_____
_____
_____
_____
_____

Brainstorming

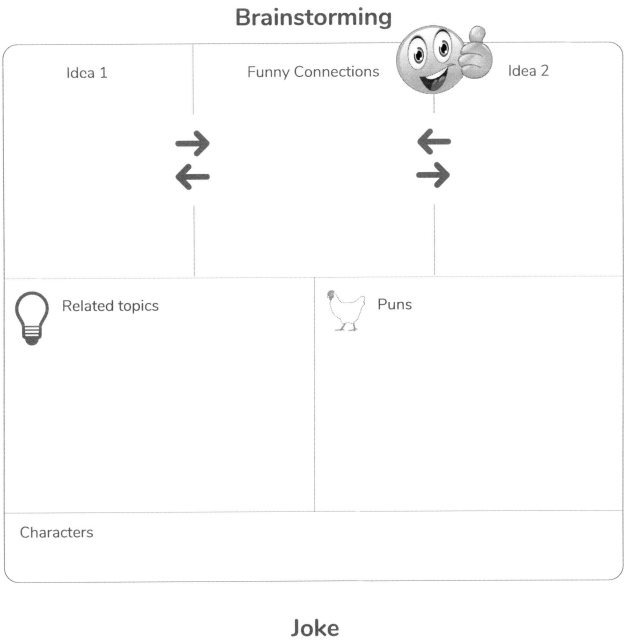

| Idea 1 | Funny Connections | Idea 2 |

Related topics

Puns

Characters

Joke

Setup

Punchline

MY JOKE OF THE DAY PLANNER

Write the joke(s) you plan to tell this week.

○ MONDAY

FUTURE JOKES

○ TUESDAY

○ WEDNESDAY

BEST JOKES THIS WEEK

○ THURSDAY

○ FRIDAY

○ SATURDAY / SUNDAY

Brainstorming

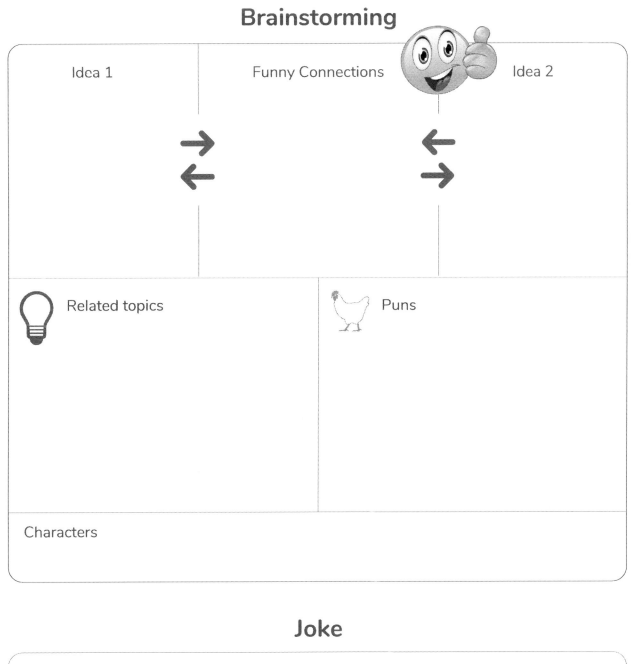

| Idea 1 | Funny Connections | Idea 2 |

Related topics

Puns

Characters

Joke

Setup

Punchline

MY JOKE OF THE DAY PLANNER

Write the joke(s) you plan to tell this week.

○ MONDAY

○ TUESDAY

○ WEDNESDAY

○ THURSDAY

○ FRIDAY

○ SATURDAY / SUNDAY

FUTURE JOKES

_____
_____
_____
_____
_____
_____

BEST JOKES THIS WEEK

_____
_____
_____
_____
_____
_____
_____
_____
_____
_____

Brainstorming

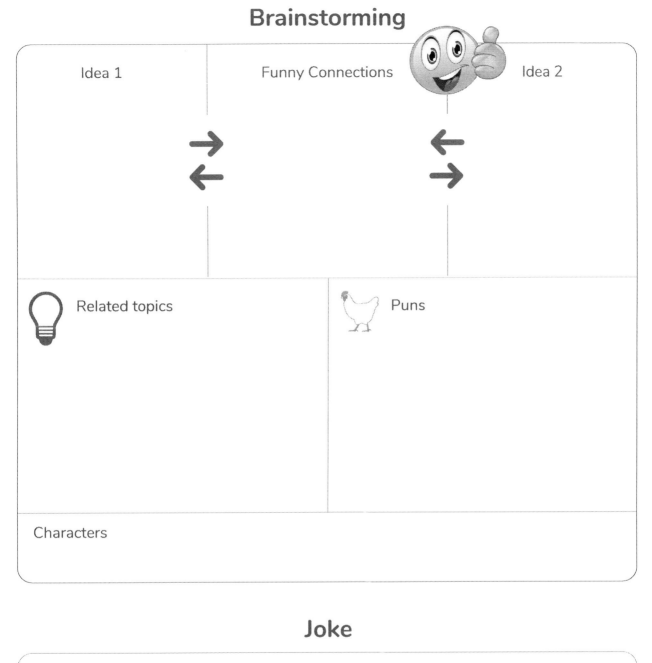

Idea 1

Funny Connections

Idea 2

Related topics

Puns

Characters

Joke

Setup

Punchline

Made in the USA
Middletown, DE
13 October 2021